See You Later, **Later,** Procrastinator!

(Get It Done)

by Pamela Espeland & Elizabeth Verdick

Illustrated by Steve Mark

free spirit
PUBLISHING®

See You Later, Procrastinator!
(Get It Done)

by Pamela Espeland & Elizabeth Verdick

Illustrated by Steve Mark

free spirit
PUBLISHING®

Library of Congress Cataloging-in-Publication Data
Espeland, Pamela.
    See you later, procrastinator! : (get it done) / by Pamela Espeland & Elizabeth Verdick ; illustrated by Steve Mark.
        p. cm. — (Laugh & learn)
    Includes bibliographical references and index.
    ISBN-13: 978-1-57542-278-7
    ISBN-10: 1-57542-278-6
 1. Procrastination—Juvenile literature. I. Verdick, Elizabeth. II. Mark, Steve. III. Title.
    BF637.P76E87 2008
    155.2'32—dc22

                                                                2007017978

eBook ISBN: 978-1-57542-820-8

Reading Level Grade 4; Interest Level Ages 8–13;
Fountas & Pinnell Guided Reading Level Q

Design by Marieka Heinlen

10 9 8 7 6 5
Printed in Hong Kong
P17201112

Free Spirit Publishing Inc.
Minneapolis, MN
(612) 338-2068
help4kids@freespirit.com
www.freespirit.com

Dedication

To Johnny,
who puts up with me
putting things off.
—PLE

To Dan, Olivia, and Zach,
who keep me laughing
and make life more fun.
—EHV

Contents

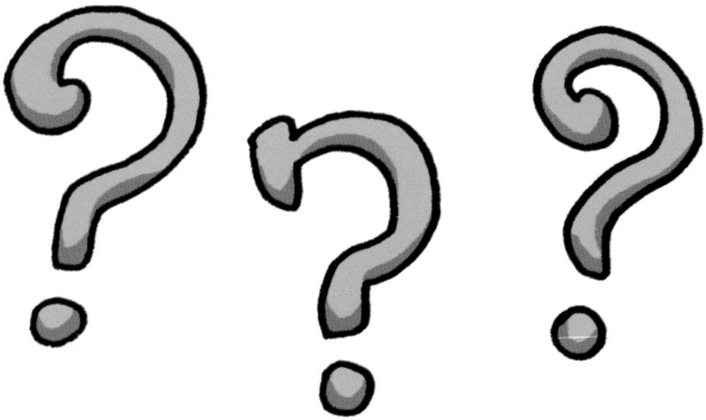

Quick Quiz

Procrastination is:

1. a small country somewhere in Europe

2. the opposite of anticrastination

3. a long word that's hard to spell

4. the habit of putting things off, doing things at the last minute, or not finishing what you start

5. I don't know—ask me later

Answer: 4.
Because 1 is silly, 2 isn't a real word, 3 is true but so what, and 5 is a joke—get it?

Procrasti-Nation

Are people always after you to get stuff done?

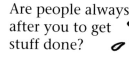

Do you often have that freaky time-is-running-out feeling?

Have you ever told a teacher "The dog ate my homework" when you don't even *have* a dog?

Do you usually wait until the last minute to start things, then panic, melt down, and blow up at everyone around you?

Do you, in a word, *procrastinate?*

Hey, join the crowd. More than 1 in every 4 Americans thinks he or she is a total procrastinator. When it comes to college students, that number rises to 3 out of 4. Young people are more likely to procrastinate than older people.

So, does it really matter if you put things off? Only if you want to live a happy, healthy life. People who procrastinate tend to be *less* happy, *less* healthy…and also less wealthy, if you care.

Chances are, someone—like a teacher or parent—has noticed that you have trouble getting things done. Perhaps that person gave you this book. Maybe you don't think you need it and you don't want to read it.

That's okay. It's not easy to admit you procrastinate and could use a little help. Maybe you *do* put stuff off now and then, or you wait and wait and wait and wait and then end up doing a pretty decent job. Is that so wrong? Of course not. Everyone procrastinates sometimes—even presidents.*

> * Andrew Jackson, the seventh President of the United States, once said, "There is no pleasure in having nothing to do; the fun is having lots to do and not doing it."

But procrastination can become a habit that's hard to break. You may get so used to it that you hardly notice when you've put stuff off—until you get that awful feeling of dread as the due date gets closer. You probably feel bad when you avoid your chores or work, think you've let someone down, or know you're going to be in trouble. It all adds up to extra stress, and who needs that?

You're growing and changing, and if you're not in middle school already, you will be soon. And middle school (or junior high) means MORE. More responsibility, more teachers, more subjects, more classrooms, more chores at home, more pressure in your after-school activities, more complicated friendships.

When you have more to stay on top of, you need habits that work *for* you, not *against* you.

That's what this book is about. It doesn't nag you, scold you, or try to make you feel bad. Instead, it tells you ways to get stuff done quickly, get organized, get control of your schedule, and most of all, get started.

For now, the only thing you need to do is keep reading.

The Pitiful Tale of Peter Procrastinator

"Great dinner, Ma," said Peter Procrastinator as he jumped up to clear the table. He made sure he was speedy so no one could get the chance to ask him about homework. The big math test was tomorrow, and he didn't want his parents to start bugging him about studying.

Soon he was parked in front of the TV, game controller in hand, thinking "Life is *good*."

Just as he reached new levels of play, his dad appeared and said, "Pardon me, Peter, but shouldn't you be doing your homework?"

"I'll get to it soon," Peter replied, not mentioning the test.

When his dad returned a half hour later, Peter was still playing. His dad held out his palm, which meant "Hand it over." Peter gave up the controller and headed to his room, but not before nabbing the phone and hiding it under his sweatshirt. He shut his bedroom door to fool his dad into thinking he was hard at work.

Peter decided to phone a few friends. They were all studying for the test and couldn't talk long. So he called his friends from another school. Then he called his cousin. "Who else can I call?" Peter wondered. Then he started dialing. "Hi, Granny, it's me! What's new?"

After all that talking, he needed a snack and went to the kitchen to make a sundae. He pulled out every ingredient he could find and built a mini-mountain of a dessert. It only took 30 minutes. Then he sat down with his parents and little sister to watch some TV.

"I really need to relax," he announced. Everyone assumed he'd finished his work, and that was just what Peter wanted them to think.

Peter watched one sitcom, then stayed seated for another. The whole family was laughing—Peter a little *too* hard. He had a weird feeling, like he was supposed to be doing something...oh, yeah, the *test*.

"I'll study in ten minutes," Peter promised himself.

"Just five more minutes, then I'll hit the books."

"I'll go when the commercials come on."

"Just a few more minutes." He glanced at the clock uneasily. It was close to bedtime.

"If a commercial for dog food comes on, *that* will be my sign to go upstairs and study."

"Fine! I'm going!"

Peter said goodnight to his family and dragged himself up to his room. He climbed into bed with his math book and a flashlight. Suddenly the math problems seemed a lot harder than he remembered. His stomach felt like a lump of cement. "Must be the ice cream," he mumbled. "Does ice cream make people sleepy…?"

Not-so-secret secret: Procrastination sure is *tiring*.

Procrastination in Action

Procrastination is a habit, which means you behave in a way that's automatic. You don't think about it, you just do it, like biting your fingernails or cracking your knuckles. You say or think things like:

"I'll do it later."

"I'll get to it tomorrow."

"It can wait."

In other words, you get in the habit of *not doing*. You may dawdle, or stall, or worry, or whine, and time ticks by. Before you know it, time has run out and you're in the hot seat. Ouch.

What happens next? You might make excuses. And making excuses—to other people or yourself—can leave you feeling like a rat.

START

"I was sick."

"I didn't know I *had* to."

"No one told me how."

"I lost it."

"I forgot."

"It wasn't my turn to do it."

"I got busy."

"I never heard you ask me."

"My cat barfed on it."

"I did most of it."

"I left it on the bus."

"I wasn't in the mood."

"I thought it was due another day."

"I didn't have time."

So, why do people procrastinate?
Good question. Can we get back to you?
Kidding.

People procrastinate for all kinds of reasons. What matters most to you (and the people around you) is why *you* procrastinate.

Time to ask yourself why.

Procrastination Investigation

To get to the bottom of your procrastination, read about each reason. Which one sounds most like you? Is there more than one? For each reason, there's a **Procrastination Buster** (**PB** for short) you can try.

RU...

WEIGHED DOWN?

Maybe you have too much to do—or you think you have too much to do. Either way, you feel buried and you don't know how to start digging out.

Pow!

Make a list of everything you think you need to do. Chores, homework, projects, tasks—everything.

Ask an adult to help you *prioritize* your list. Put an A next to things that are super important, a B next to things that are less important, and a C next to things that can wait.

Finally (and this is the fun part) *cross out* anything you really *don't* need to do. You know, things you've been meaning to do for weeks or months and never got around to. Or things it's now too late to do. Or things that simply don't matter anymore.

Look—your list just got shorter. Can you pick *one* of your A or B priorities and get it done (or at least start it) today?

GROSSED OUT?

Some tasks are just plain disgusting. Does anyone really *enjoy* scooping out the litter box or cleaning off the blobs of toothpaste stuck to the sink? Who wants to take out the smelly trash or pick up doggy doo-doo?

Zap!

Hold your nose, grit your teeth, and get it done. (Be sure to wash your hands after.) Sorry, but that's the only way 'cause if it's your job and *you* don't do it, who will? For majorly stinky tasks, tie a bandanna over your nose and mouth. If you're working outdoors, make sure the neighbors know you're not a bandit.

STRESSED OUT?

Maybe you procrastinate when a project seems too difficult. If learning a long list of spelling words is hard for you, then you may get stressed when you think of the task ahead. Have you ever noticed that the longer you put off learning the list, the longer the list seems to become?

Slam!

Slice your big, difficult project into smaller, easier tasks. Some people call this the *salami technique*. For example, if you're supposed to learn 15 spelling words, make 3 lists of 5 words each, then learn one list at a time. (Learn it, don't eat it.) For more about long-term projects, go to page 72.

TOO BLASÉ?*

* Impress all your friends with this word. It means "bored with life." Say *blah-ZAY*.

Maybe you think, "What's the point of doing homework?" Or "Why bother doing chores?" Or "So what if I clean my room? It'll just get dirty again."

What you need is a *motivator.* A motivator is something you want and are willing to work for. It's a reward you give yourself for a job well done (a bonus, not a bribe). Pick things that are fun and that you don't get to do every day.

Bang!

An allowance can be a motivator. Talk to the adults at home to see if you can earn an allowance for doing chores. (But you really have to *do* the chores to get the cash.) With help from your family, you can come up with a list of daily and weekly chores, a fair amount for your allowance, and maybe even ways to earn extra money for extra work. Make a chore chart (see page 66) so you remember what you're expected to do. Some families like to encourage kids to divide their allowance into thirds: save a third, donate a third to a worthy cause, and spend a third on things you want to buy. Go to pages 38–39 for more motivators.

WORN OUT?

Do you ever start stuff with a BANG but then just... lose...steam? This can happen with big projects that have a lot of steps or take a long time to complete. It's easy to lose interest or get stuck. Even if you sizzle and fizzle, you don't have to give up.

Bam!

Know your "prime time." When do you work best? When are you most alert? For some people, it's first thing in the morning. For others, it's later in the day. Experiment to find out when you're at your peak. Right after school? After dinner? The moment you wake up? Saturday mornings before seeing your friends?

FREAKED OUT?

Have you ever had a dream where a monster was chasing you but you couldn't move a muscle? Fear can freeze you into doing nothing. It's a major reason why people procrastinate.

There are all kinds of fears. Maybe you're...

Scared to Fail

Fear Fact #1: Nobody succeeds at everything.

Fear Fact #2: Everybody fails sometimes.

It helps to have a *role model*—someone to look up to. When it comes to failure, the American inventor Thomas Edison (think *the light bulb*) is a terrific role model. Along the way, he had many failures, but he kept a positive attitude. "I have not failed," he once said. "I've just found 10,000 ways that won't work."

 Look around for a role model. This can be someone you know or someone you've heard about or read about. It can be a kid in your class who has her act together, or a kid in your neighborhood who always seems on top of things. It can even be a made-up character from a book or movie. Think about why you admire that person.

Scared of Mistakes

Fear Fact #3: The world won't end if you make a mistake.

Fear Fact #4: Perfection isn't possible.

Some experts believe that half of everything we learn comes from making mistakes. You weren't born knowing how to walk, talk, or feed yourself. You fell down, said lots of nonsense words, and dropped food all over the floor (okay, maybe you still do). But what if you stopped trying the first time any of those "mistakes" happened? Well, for one thing, you'd probably still be in diapers.

Ka-bam!

Instead of seeing mistakes as failures, see them as something you *learned from.* What would you have done differently? How might you do better next time?

Scared to Decide

Fear Fact #5: Not deciding *is* deciding.
(Did you ever think of it that way?)

Ka-Pow!

Got a decision to make? Toss a coin or do eeny-meeny-miney-mo. Or write things you need to do on slips of paper, put them in a hat, mix them up, and pull one out without peeking first.

Scared to Succeed

Maybe you're used to being kind of lazy. Maybe the people around you don't expect much from you. Sometimes, you might even have weird thoughts, like "If I succeed, people will want me to do it all the time." Or "What if they think I've changed too much? What if they get jealous? What if they tease me about being a show-off or a nerd?"

Fear Fact #6: You're not really afraid of success. You're afraid of what might happen if you succeed.

Boom!

List the *worst* things that can happen if you succeed. Then list the *best* things. If you still don't think it's good to give something your best try, share your lists with someone you trust. Fear of success will keep you from succeeding in life.

Just Plain Scared

It may sound strange, but sometimes people put off doing things they're dying to do.

Have you ever decided to wait instead of trying out for a team, talking to a girl or boy you like, or sharing your talents with an audience? When you're scared, you might grab hold of *any* excuse, like "My horoscope was bad today" or "I might miss something good on TV."

Fear Fact #7: Sometimes, when you avoid something scary, you lose out on a chance to shine or have fun.

Bonk!

Write down something you've been putting off. Then write down the reason. What are you afraid of? Is there someone you can talk to about your fear? Could you (with help) take a deep breath and face your fear?

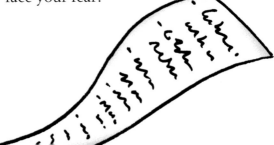

RU...

FED UP?

Sometimes it's a pain being a kid. Parents, teachers, coaches, and other adults tell you what to do—a lot. Most adults are big on rules, homework, chores, and bedtimes. Don't you sometimes wish *you* could order *them* around?

The thing is, grown-ups are in charge, and they usually want what's best for you. The reason they make you do things is not to make you miserable, but to help you learn and grow.

Sock!

List some funny rules you'd come up with if you were the adult. Like "School is optional," "It's against the law to serve Brussels sprouts," and "Kids can stay up as late as they want." Laughter can be a motivator. It lightens your mood and adds more fun to your life.

BUMMED OUT?

Maybe you've put off apologizing to a friend or writing a card for someone who's sick. Perhaps you've been working on getting in shape or fitting in better at school, but you think you're not making progress.

At times like these, worries or sadness can get in the way. Procrastinating might give you a little lift—a brief sense of relief. But don't let yourself fall into the procrastination trap. That feeling of "Good, I don't have to deal with it!" won't last. You'll feel better if you take a deep breath and just do what you have to do.

Thwack!

Talk with an adult you trust about your worries or sadness. Ask for help if you need it. No matter how bad you feel, you're not alone, and someone out there cares and will listen.

SPACED OUT?

A lot of kids procrastinate because they don't know what else to do. No one has ever taught them how to plan ahead, make good choices, and get things done. They get discouraged because they don't know where or how to start. Or they get off to a good start but don't know what to do next. Help!

Yum!

Fix yourself a sandwich and keep reading. One way to get rid of the procrastination habit is to replace it with great new habits that help you feel more in charge of your life. That's what you're about to do.

20 Ways to Kiss Procrastination Good-Bye

Don't worry—you don't have to learn all 20 ways at once. And you don't have to learn them in any order. Take your time and ask for help when you need it.

1. Take a Chill Pill

This book isn't about turning you into a Super Kid who always gets everything done on time and never goofs off. Who wants to live like *that?*

Don't sit around thinking you're a loser because you're not great at starting or finishing stuff. Maybe you're having trouble at home because your family isn't organized or doesn't have much time for you. Maybe you're struggling in school because you're bored or confused, or don't understand what your teacher expects of you. It's possible you procrastinate because you now have bigger responsibilities you don't know how to handle.

If you want to make changes, you can. If you think you can't do it on your own, get help. Go to an adult you trust—a parent, other relative, teacher, or school counselor. You might say something like "I feel stuck and need some help," or "School is hard for me. What can I do?" Just saying those words is a start.

Now relax for a moment. Think about a time when you accomplished something you really wanted to do. Maybe you read a long book and wrote a great report on it. Maybe you reached a goal in a sport or an activity, or helped organize a volunteer project with your class. Perhaps you learned a new piece of music, planned a party, or made something you're proud of.

Whatever it was—*you* did it. Which means you can kick the procrastination habit, too.

Time to say...

"See you later, procrastinator!"

"Buh-bye, putter-offer!"

"Hit the road, dawdler!"

"Sayonara, slowpoke!"

Make up other funny ways to say farewell to your inner slacker.

2. Mission: Organization

Getting organized is one of the BEST ways to get your act together. Lucky it's not Mission: Impossible.

Even the worst clutter bunny can learn to get organized. It's the only way to avoid the dreaded *Domino Effect.* *

* That's when you stand a row of dominos on end, knock over the first one, and they all fall down.

Must write birthday thank-you notes.

Did anyone keep a list?

What did I get again?

Stationery. Oh yeah, got some for my b-day.

Pen. Uh, do I have one?

Now, where did I put it?

Got one. Oops, no ink.

How do you get organized? It doesn't happen all in one day. It's something you may need to work on bit by bit. Some areas of your life may be more organized than others, so you'll want to take a look at where you need the most help. For example, are you pretty organized at home but not at school? Or maybe it's the other way around. Do you need help in both areas? Check out pages 42–44, 50–51, and 56–57.

3. Get a Plan, Man

You've got a busy brain and a body full of energy. You have boundless imagination, random thoughts, and wild and crazy dreams. It's easy to get distracted and completely forget about what you're *supposed* to do. That's where a **planner** comes in handy.

A planner is a great tool for keeping track of your daily tasks and activities. Perhaps your school already provides one. If you don't have a planner, you can buy one at an office supplies store.

October 22-24

22 Monday

Social Studies—
Finish Chapter 5 ✓

Math homework ✓

4pm Soccer ✓
practice

A good basic one is a **weekly planner**. When you open it up, you see a whole week at-a-glance. Each column shows the date and day, and there's lots of room for filling in things like:

- homework assignments

- test dates

- special projects

- after-school practices and events

- chores

- family activities

- time for play, fun, and relaxation

October 25-28

Thursday **25**

Spelling quiz

Science Worksheet due

4pm Soccer practice

Work on art project

Friday **26**

6pm family picnic

Activit

It's best to write in your planner with a pencil. Activities and assignments can change, and you may need to erase something you've written. You can check off tasks after you've completed them. (Checking off tasks feels *SO* good.) If you want, put stars or stickers next to special dates or events. That way, you'll be sure to notice them.

As a middle school or junior high student (or a soon-to-be one), you've got more classes and activities to keep track of. That's why a planner is so useful. When you have a written record of what you have to do, it's easier to follow through.

October 22-24

29 Monday

Media center day

5:30 Piano Lesson

Work on Science project ✓

30 Tuesday
Math worksheet due

✓ Look at your planner every morning before school.

✓ Check it again toward the end of the school day.

✓ Bring your planner home with you.

✓ Look at it again in the evening. Have you accomplished what you needed to do?

✓ If you didn't finish something, write down *when* you'll do it.

✓ If you need a motivator, see the list on pages 38–39.

P.S. You may hear people say, "A job well done is its own reward." PUH-lease! If that were true, people wouldn't need motivators. Or paychecks.

3pm Chess Club

Clean hamster cage

October 25-28

Thursday

1

Finish Science Project!!

Mighty Motivators and Fun Rewards

- ✳ watch a movie you love, even if you've seen it a zillion times

- ✳ rent or buy a new video game you've been wanting

- ✳ throw a party to celebrate reaching a goal

- ✳ invite people over for karaoke or dancing

- ✳ get new supplies for your favorite sport, hobby, or craft

* go somewhere fun with your family: mini-golf, a water park, a museum

* go to dinner at your family's favorite restaurant

* make a special meal with all your favorite foods

* plan to visit a friend you don't often get to see

* buy what you've been saving your allowance for

* host an outdoor event for your friends: a softball or kickball game, badminton tournament, water balloon fight, obstacle course, wacky races

* earn certificates for something fun or special, like you get breakfast in bed (but you have to make these certificates ahead of time with a parent who can let you choose one when you've reached a goal, finished a tough task, or earned a reward)

4. Just Do It

When you're faced with a task you keep putting off, don't want to do, or can't seem to start:

Do the **worst** part first.
The rest will be a breeze.

OR...

Do the **easy** part first.
It's an instant win.

You're right. Those are *total opposites.* That's because there's really no *best* way to beat procrastination that works for everyone. Just do what works for you.

5. To-Do-Be-Do-Be-Do

No matter how brainy you may be, it's hard to remember everything you want or need to do. And no wonder: Your head is brimming with more interesting things, like…

your dreams

and daydreams

and facts you learn in school

and conversations you had with friends

and jokes you heard

and tips from your teachers and coaches

and funny things your dog did

and plans for after school

and weird-but-true stories

and questions about life

Get the picture? There's not much room left over for boring stuff like "Sort my socks."

A **To-Do list** solves that problem. You can use the list *in addition to* your planner. The list is for tasks that suddenly come up or are extras in your day. So, if you need to wash your sports uniform before the next practice, you'd put that on your list. If you have to email Uncle Ozzy, add it to the list. If you need a reminder to get new glue—you guessed it, put it on the list.

To-Do lists should be simple. Not like this:

✓ make breakfast

✓ eat breakfast

✓ chew each bite carefully

✓ swallow

✓ drink juice

✓ wipe mouth

You don't have to list *everything* you do in a day. Just put down a few basics—things you're likely to forget or put off till later.

✳ Make a quick list every day.

✳ Check things off (or cross them off) as you go.

✳ Give yourself little rewards (like 15 minutes of computer or skateboarding time) when you get stuff done.

✳ Add any items that *aren't* checked off to your next day's list.

6. Psych Yourself Up

When you can't get started:

- **Think** about how good you'll feel when you're DONE with the task, not how awful it will be to do it.

- **Ask** yourself, "What will happen if I get it done?" Then ask yourself, "What will happen *to me* if I *don't* get it done?" Is it worth getting in trouble or getting a poor grade?

- **Tell** yourself you'll do the task for just 5 minutes. Set a timer and start. When the timer goes off, stop.

When you can't keep going:

- **Look** at what you've already done. Congratulate yourself for getting that far.

- **Take** a short break—10 to 15 minutes at the most. Do something you enjoy, or something that gives you energy. Run around the block? Shoot hoops? Jump up and down?

- **Play** beat-the-clock. Estimate how long it will take you to get the job done. Then set a timer and GO GO GO!

7. Have a Few Tricks Up Your Sleeve

A lot of times, people don't really mean to procrastinate. They just forget to do what they're supposed to do.

So *you* don't forget, try these memory tricks.

- **Tie a string around your finger.** This is an old-fashioned way to remember something. (The string is your reminder.)

- **Write it on your palm or the back of your hand.** Same idea as the string thing. (Don't use permanent ink or you'll have to look at it for days.)

- **Put a pebble in your shoe.** Do this before you go to bed at night. When you put your shoe on in the morning, you'll feel the pebble and this will jog your memory.

- **Become an elephant.** An elephant never forgets.

How will you remember what it is you're supposed to remember? Write yourself a note or add an item to your To-Do list.

Meet
Evan
@ 6pm!!

Ways to sharpen your memory:

✓ **Write it down.** When you write things down you're more likely to remember them. And even if you forget them, you'll have a written reminder.

✓ **Mix it up.** When you're learning something new, learn it in different ways. Read it aloud, sing it, draw it, dance it, map it. Make up rhymes about it.

✓ **Talk it out.** If your mind is crowded with fears and worries, tell an adult you trust.

✓ **Ditch distractions.** A lot of people think they can *multitask* (do a bunch of things at once). But it's hard to concentrate when you're watching TV and listening to music and surfing the Web and texting and IMing and chatting and playing video games. It just is. Try to focus on one thing at a time.

✓ **Laugh it up.** You'll remember things longer if you link them to something funny.

✓ **Move it or lose it.** When there's something you need to remember, say it out loud to yourself while walking, jumping, or throwing a ball.

✓ **Eat red foods.** They're rich in beta carotene, which is good for your memory. Some examples are strawberries, tomatoes, red cabbage, radishes, watermelon, cherries. Not on the list: red M&Ms.

✓ **Stick 'em up.** Write reminders on sticky notes and put them where you'll see them—your mirror, your locker, your notebook.

Bring treats on Monday

Fold & put away my laundry!

Fill water bottles before practice

EAT Strawberries

Science test Science test... forget the rest!

TV TONIGHT

Walk Barkley

8. Rooty-Toot Routines

Weird but true: Routines give you F-R-E-E-D-O-M. They make life simpler. For example, you probably have a shower routine—one you may not even notice. Think about it: Do you always start at the top by washing your hair? Or do you begin feet first and work your way up? Whatever your routine may be, you can probably complete it when you're half asleep.

By coming up with routines you can count on, you'll make your life easier and more organized. Here are some good ones to practice:

Morning routine: Wash up. Get dressed. Eat healthy, nutritious breakfast. Brush teeth. Look at planner. Check backpack.

End-of-school-day routine: Look at planner. Gather textbooks, library books, folders, assignments, jacket, activity/sporting gear, etc. Bring backpack home.

Homework routine: Review assignments. Plan the time it will take to finish them. Get a healthy snack and a glass of water (for energy). Work in a quiet area. Stretch every so often. Have an adult check your work.

Bedtime routine: Pack backpack. Choose clothes for next day. Review planner and To-Do list. Wash up. Brush teeth. Look forward to tomorrow.

Once you have your routines memorized, it's a no-brainer to get them done.

9. Beat Boredom

When something is dreadful or dull, you could…

Get out the music. Some people believe that music by Mozart can make you smarter. But you can listen to whatever you like, depending on what you're doing. If you're studying, it's probably best to choose music without words so the lyrics don't distract you.

Get a friend or family member to help you. Almost any task is easier (and more fun) when you do it with someone else.

Get someone else to do it. This is called *delegating,* and adults do it all the time. Of course, it depends on the task. You can't get someone else to memorize the multiplication tables for you. And you *do* need to do your own homework. But you can see if a sibling is willing to do your wastebasket-emptying or bed-making for a day or two. (What will you do for him or her?)

Get fired up. Setting the table for dinner is not the most exciting thing in the world. So *make* it exciting. Can you use the special placemats? What about candles or homemade place cards?

10. Tick-Tock-Tick

Most procrastinators are very good at finding fun and interesting ways to waste time. How about you? Do you get carried away making coo-tie catchers* or little paper foot-balls? Do you ever decide that you *just have to* organize your entire collection of baseball cards, even though you have a lot of homework?

* You know, those folded-up paper fortune-teller thingies.

Do hours go by as you make weird faces in the mirror, balance pencils on your nose, and count your freckles?

Keeping an eye on the time helps you not waste time. Some of the biggest time eaters have screens: TVs, computers, handheld video game players, and cell phones. The hours can slip away when you're online, watching the tube, playing video/computer games, or texting your friends.

But that doesn't mean these activities are bad. You just have to set some limits. If your mom or dad already sets limits for you, be sure to stick to them.

For example, you could give yourself 45 minutes to an hour of screen time per day (if that's what your parents say is okay). That could mean one TV show and around a half hour of surfing the Web. Or you could do a few 15-minute sessions of video games.

Figure out how to fit these times around your other activities. It may help to set a timer or have a family member remind you when your time is up.

If you don't have a watch, start saving up to buy one. You'll be able to keep track of the time and how long it takes you to do stuff. You could even get one with a built-in alarm that beeps to remind you of important events.

Talking on the phone with friends is fun, but you don't have to talk forever. If some of your friends are super chatty, just tell them you've got a 15-minute limit to every phone call.

Do you give yourself enough time each day to relax? Don't forget to stare out the window, play with your pet, stretch your body, talk about nothing, and read for the fun of it.

Total Time Wasters

- talking on the phone with someone you don't really want to talk to about something you don't really care about

- watching repeats of TV shows you've already seen a bunch of times

- preparing for an hour to do a task that takes five minutes

- mindless Web surfing or IMing (if your eyes are glazed over and you're drooling on the keyboard, it's been too long)

- eating a lot of junk food as a way to put off doing something you're supposed to do *(gulp)*

- playing a video game that you've already reached the highest level on so many times you could play it with your eyes closed

- trying to work when you're just too tired (take a nap or get a good night's sleep, then try again)

11. Know Your Mess

If you're lucky enough to have your own bedroom, you probably see it as YOUR space where you do everything: sleep, dress, read, hang out, do homework, talk with friends, and secretly try out your latest dance moves. Your room may tell the story of your life with photos, cards, trophies or awards, yearbooks, magazines, half-finished projects, posters, and more. Your room may be home to pets and plants. It could be the place where you've saved nearly everything you've ever owned. Is this okay? YES!*

Being surrounded by stuff that has meaning to you can be comforting. It helps you define who you are. It's fun to glance up and see pictures or objects that leave you happy and peaceful. It's cool to look around and feel at home. But if you constantly lose stuff in the clutter or lose energy every time you walk into your room, that should tell you something. What kind of mess do you really have?

* Unless your room drives your family crazy. Talk to them about that.

- Is your floor a giant pile of clothing?

- Do you sometimes trip over your own stuff?

- Is the dust so thick you can see your cat's paw prints in it?

- Do you find old, moldy food in places other than the trashcan?

- Is there a funky smell when you walk in?

- Do people enter and say "Ewww"?

If you answered *yes* to any of these questions, it may be time to address that mess.

Having a neater space can help you procrastinate less because you won't have as many distractions. You'll be more organized. And you'll feel more in control.

See the next page for tips on how to start.

12. The Amazing Race

The bad news is, it's time to clean your room.

The good news is, it doesn't have to take long. In fact, you can do it in *just 15 minutes*.

Before the official countdown, find:

✓ a timer

✓ your favorite music

✓ a clothes hamper

✓ a trashcan (bonus points for lining it with a plastic bag first)

✓ a basket or box for collecting clutter

✓ another basket or box for gathering games, music, and other stuff worth keeping

✓ the vacuum cleaner

✓ a cloth and cleaner for wiping surfaces

For fun, challenge yourself to see how fast you can find what you need.

GET READY:

Set your timer for 15 minutes, then put on your music as loud as you're allowed. Find a way to keep this book propped open so you can quickly look at the list of tasks on pages 60–62 as you clean.

GET GOING:
Do these 10 tasks.*
Do them FAST.

1. Deal with the dirty clothes. Put the laundry in the hamper or down the chute. (Don't just grab *all* the clothes whether they're dirty or not. Whoever does the laundry will be mad.) If you want an extra challenge, turn all the inside-out clothes right side out.

* You can get the job done quicker if you ask a friend or sibling to give you a hand.

2. Trash the trash. Scrape old food into the garbage can, toss your candy wrappers, dispose of your wadded-up gum, get rid of used tissues, and throw out stuff that's broken or useless.

3. Make your bed. Pull up the sheets, straighten the blankets, smooth out the bedspread. If you have a lot of stuffed animals or pillows for your bed, put them in place.

4. Do your desk. Stack your papers, quickly arrange your supplies, put items in your backpack. Grab the cloth and cleaning solution and give your desk a wipe-down.

5. Clear clutter. There's probably stuff in your room that belongs somewhere else. Like: Dishes go to the kitchen, your brother's games go in his room, the dog toys belong with the dog. Collect all these items in one of the baskets or boxes.

6. Clean up the keepers. Look at the floor and furniture. If you've got toys, games, books, electronics, hobby items, pictures, and other stuff that's yours to keep, then collect them in the other basket or box. This isn't where they'll stay—you can put them away another time. For now, just get them off the furniture and floor. Take the cleaning cloth and wipe your dresser and nightstand.

7. Clean up your clean clothes. Pick up anything that's clean, whether it's draped over a chair or on your closet floor. Put these clothes on your bed. If you're fast at folding, fold them and stack them to put away later. Hang up items that might wrinkle.

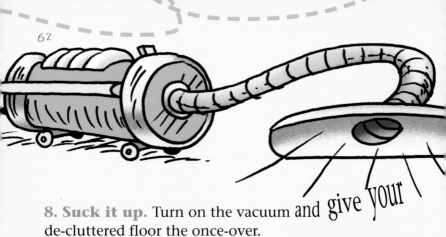

8. Suck it up. Turn on the vacuum and give your de-cluttered floor the once-over.

9. Store your supplies. Put the vacuum and cleaning supplies away. Take out the trash. Return the hamper to its place. You can put your two baskets or boxes in a corner until you're ready to deal with them.

10. Pat yourself on the back. You did it! You got a great start on a hard job. Now kick back and enjoy your space. You don't have to turn into a neat freak, but you'll feel calmer and more focused when your room is clean. You might even decide to keep it that way.

Later today, empty those baskets/boxes by putting each item back where it belongs. Make it a game by setting the timer to see if you can do the task in less than 5 or 10 minutes. You can even plan a reward for yourself afterward, like playing outside or calling a friend.

If you share a room with a sloppy sibling, show this list to him or her. Offer to help with the cleanup.

13. Cut the Clutter

Are you a pack rat? Are your room, desk at school, locker, sports bag, and backpack filled with things you don't want, need, or even remember? To avoid pack-rattyness, nibble on these steps.

1. Go through your stuff a shelf at a time, a box at a time, a drawer at a time, or a heap at a time. Don't try to do this all at once or you may give up before you really get started. (You might write "Go through stuff in backpack" or "Go through stuff on closet floor" on your To-Do list.)

2. Sort things into two piles: **Keep** and **Don't Keep**.

3. Put the **Keeps** away.

4. Decide what to do with the **Don't Keeps**. Like:

   - return them (if you borrowed them)

   - give them to a friend

   - hand them down to a younger sibling

   - donate items that are clean and usable

   - recycle what you can

If you end up with a lot of **Don't Keeps** that are still in good shape, get together with friends and have a yard or garage sale. (Try not to buy each other's stuff.)

5. If you can't decide if something is a **Keep** or a **Don't Keep**, try this: Put it in a box, write today's date on the outside, and seal the box with tape. Put the box someplace safe. Three months from now (or six months, if you can wait that long), open the box. If you haven't missed or needed what's inside, it's a **Don't Keep**.

Whenever you get something NEW, get rid of something OLD. This prevents clutter from building up and taking over.

14. Chart Those Chores

To remember everything you're supposed to do, you'd have to grow a second head. A better idea would be to chart your daily or weekly chores. That way, you can check your chart instead of procrastinating or being reminded to feed the parakeet, sort your laundry, rake the yard, or whatever.

Ask a family grown-up to help you chart your chores. Start by making a list of what you're expected to do around the house. Then decide what days you're supposed to do each chore.

Skippy goes to the vet this FRIDAY

Chore	Sunday	Monday	Tuesday	Wednesday	Thursday	Friday	Saturday
Set table for dinner		X		X		X	
Load & unload dishwasher	X		X		X		X
Take Skippy for his walk		X		X		X	
Clean room				X			
Sweep steps					X		

remember...
Send Grandma a thank-you note!

If you want, you can decorate your chore chart with funny drawings, cartoons, or pictures cut out of magazines. Make a new chart every week or month—as often as you need to. Then *use* it (don't ignore it).

You'll feel more organized, and you'll get stuff done.

LIAR, LIAR, PANTS ON FIRE

Procrastinators tell a lot of tall tales. Like these:

"It will take too long." **The truth:** It will probably take *less* time than you think it will. And you may spend *more* time worrying and complaining and making excuses. (In the 10 minutes you spend arguing with your mom about why you can't do the dishes, you could finish doing the dishes.)

"It'll be easier later." **The truth:** Smelly garbage smells worse on the second day. Homework doesn't get easier if you put it off.

"I'm way too busy right now." **The truth:** Sometimes staying busy is a disguise for procrastinating. If you're reorganizing your backpack for the fifth time this week, you may think you're not procrastinating. BUT if you have a big test tomorrow, you need this time to study. (**Tip:** Mind your busy-ness.)

"I need to help my friend." **The truth:** Helping a friend is a good thing. Ignoring your own responsibilities isn't. Get your work done first, then use your leftover time to help a friend.

"I work best under pressure." **The truth:** Last-minute work is hardly ever your best work. Plus, all that pressure = too much stress.

Instead of tall tales, tell yourself the truth. If you need to pump yourself up to get things done, take another look at pages 40–41, 45–46, and 52.

15. Homework Helpers

Quick—
name the one thing almost every
student puts off doing.

you guessed it: Homework.

Homework is here to stay, so you might as well find ways to stop procrastinating. Here's what you need to do the job.

Quiet. Find a quiet place to work. Turn off the TV or music, and tell your family you don't want to be disturbed.

Space. Work at a desk with a comfy chair. Make sure you have good lighting so you don't strain your eyes. Have all the materials you need within reach: paper, pens, pencils, glue, markers, a stapler, paperclips, and so on.

Energy boosters. Work at a time when you know you can focus (like after school or dinner). Drink water and eat healthy snacks if you're hungry. Get up and stretch every 10 or 15 minutes so your legs don't fall asleep.

Good habits. Do the hardest homework first to get it out of the way. (Or the easiest. See pages 40–41.) Always read the directions carefully so you know exactly what to do. If you have any doubts about the assignment, ask a parent or call a friend in your class. Do the work neatly so your teacher can read it.

Questions. *Ask* them. It's frustrating to struggle through work you don't understand. Find a parent or another adult helper. If this isn't possible for whatever reason, write down your questions and ask your teacher the next day. Explain that you tried the assignment but had trouble. (It's better to admit it than to make up a crazy excuse.)

The finishing touch. When you're done, check over your work. Ask a parent or another adult to double-check it. Last but not least, put your homework in your folder so it doesn't get wrinkled, then load it in your backpack.

Ta-da! You're done!

16. Big Project?
Break It Down

You've probably heard grown-ups say "Got a big project? Break it down into smaller parts." And maybe you've thought, "Sounds good, but what does that *mean*? How exactly am I supposed to do it?"

Every project is different, but here are some basic steps that can help you get started and get your project done on time (or sooner).

- **Start planning on the same day you get the assignment.**

- **Make sure you understand what you're supposed to do.** What will the end product look like? A report? A display? A performance? A chart? A model of the Pyramids? If you don't understand, ask your teacher.

- **Make a To-Do list of everything you need to do to complete your project.** Prioritize your list. What will you need to do first? Second? Third? Write a number by each item on your list, then rewrite your list in order. (Remember, you get to *cross things off* as you finish them. Wa-hoo!)

- **Make a list of any materials you'll need to complete your project.** Are there some you already have? How will you get the ones you don't have? Will you need to use a computer?

- **Decide if you'll need help from your parents or other adults.** Will you need people to take you to the library, the office supplies store, or a museum? Ask them to help you, and let them know when you'll need their help. (Don't wait until the last minute. Parents *hate* that.)

- **Set deadlines for finishing each step of your project.** Write them in your planner.

- **Schedule a certain time each day to work on your project.** Write it in your planner. Stick with your plan.

What if you miss a day? Don't give up or tell yourself the whole plan is ruined (it's not). Get back to your project on the very next day.

When you take time to plan a project, it takes less time to do than if you just jump in. Try saying this five times fast: Proper Planning Prevents Poor Performance.*

* Without spitting.

17. Don't Be a Blockhead

Do you ever have a writing assignment and just... can't...get...started? You stare at the blank paper, you fill it with little doodles, you sit there and sit there, and *nothing*. Or you stare at the computer screen, hypnotized by the blinking cursor and...*zilch*. You're not procrastinating—even if people think you are. You've got a case of **writer's block**. Here's how to un-block it.

- **Don't panic!** Spend a few minutes reading a cartoon book, the comics section of the newspaper, or a funny story. This may put you in the mood to write.

- **Free write.** Put pencil to paper (or fingers to keyboard) and write anything. Even if it's "Help! I have writer's block! Help! Oh, help!" Keep writing for 5 to 10 minutes.

- **Forget grammar, spelling, punctuation, and all the other rules.** You can fix your writing later. Just get some ideas on the page.

- **Copy a few paragraphs or pages from your favorite book.** Or imitate your favorite writer's style. But wait—this is just *practice*. Don't copy someone else's writing for your *real* assignment. That's cheating.

- **Write the ending first.** Or the middle. You don't have to start at the beginning. But once you *get* going, it's easier to *keep* going.

- **Relax! Daydream for a few moments.** Take a break. The more you worry about writer's block, the harder it is to beat it.

18. Picture Your Success

Sometimes you can't get started. Sometimes you start and get stuck. What to do? Close your eyes and *see* yourself doing a task or project from beginning to end.

Many athletes use this method, called *visualization,* before they compete. Visualization means creating a mental image of what you want to happen. Sports reporters and fans have watched top athletes close their eyes and go through the motions of a race, a gymnastics routine, or a golf swing. It looks weird, but who cares? It works!

More mind games:

- **Think back on a success, then give it a name.** You raked the yard in 15 minutes flat and your dad was so impressed he took you to a movie? You might name that "Whirlwind." You were the only person in your class to ace the spelling test? That could be a "Webster."* You did something that took strength and energy and a refusal to give up? You "Mad-Dogged-It." Your name becomes your *trigger word* for a task. Think or say the word and it snaps you into the right mindset.

  * For Noah Webster, the dictionary guy.

- **Calm yourself and clear your mind before starting a task.** To calm yourself, take a few deep breaths. *In…out…in…out…in…out.* To clear your mind, try a mini-meditation. Find a comfy place to sit, close your eyes, and think a single word or syllable over and over and over again. *Umbrella… umbrella…umbrella.* Do this for 3 to 5 minutes.

- **Give yourself a pep talk.** Tell yourself, "I know I can do this." "I will do it really well." "I feel good." "I am confident and capable." "When I'm done, I am *so* going to celebrate!"

19. Shoulda Woulda Gotta

How many times have you told yourself:

"I should start my homework now."

"I gotta get this assignment done by tomorrow."

"I'm supposed to sweep the floor."

"I have to walk the dog."

"I need to clear the table after dinner."

Should, gotta, supposed to, have to, need to, must. No wonder you don't wanna! What if you said:

"I choose to start my homework now."

"I want to get this assignment done before tomorrow."

"I'm going to sweep that floor until it shines!"

"I'd *love* to walk the dog."

"I can't wait to be done clearing the table."

Feel the difference? Changing your words can help you change your mind.

Instead of this:	Say this:
"Someday, I'll…"	"On Monday, I'll…"
"I can't…"	"I can try…"
"I wish…"	"I could…"
"I might…"	"I will…"
"I'm going to HATE doing this."	"I'm going to feel GREAT when I'm done."

While you're at it, get off your **BUT** and stand on your **AND**.

Instead of this:	Say this:
"BUT I don't want to!"	"AND I'll do it!"
"BUT it's too hard!"	"AND I know I can do it!"
"BUT I'm too busy!"	"AND I'll get it done!"
"BUT I want to go outside and play!"	"AND I'll do my work first, then have fun!"

Try to stop making excuses, because excuses are little lies. Believe it or not, it's better to be honest and face the consequences. A teacher who hears, "Mrs. S., I didn't finish my report yet. I tried, but I got confused and I could use some extra help," is more likely to be understanding. A parent who hears, "I know you asked me to do that, but I was thinking about other stuff and it slipped my mind," is more likely to give you a second chance. Try it and see.

20. Goals Get You There

A *goal* is something you work toward. Ideally, it's something *you* want, not something other people think you should want. But you can also set goals to accomplish things you need to do or have to do…or else.

When you set goals, think SPAM. Good goals are:

Specific

Positive

Active

Manageable

A goal that's *specific* tells you exactly what you want to accomplish in a certain time frame:

My goal is to work on my jump shot three afternoons this week.

A goal that's *positive* says what you'll do, not what you have to stop doing (so you feel good about trying):

I will start my homework right after dinner tonight.

Doesn't that feel better than "I'll stop being a bum and putting off my homework"?

A goal that's *active* includes an action word. Make sure you put at least one verb or "do it" word in there:

> I'll **gather** all my dirty clothes, then **ask** Dad to **teach** me how to **work** the washing machine.

A goal that's *manageable* is within your reach:

> I'll practice my music lessons for 15 minutes longer during each session this week.

That's more realistic than "I'll learn that new piece of music if it's the last thing I ever do!"

Try setting some SPAM goals that can help you get tasks done, finish a project you've started, or make positive changes in your life. This is a powerful way to kick the procrastination habit.

Once you've got a goal, give it the "sniff test." Is it **S**pecific, **P**ositive, **A**ctive, and **M**anageable? To see if you know the difference between a sweet goal and a stinker, try the test on the next page.

Directions: Find the stinkers:

I'll study my vocabulary words for 20 minutes after dinner.

I'll get an A++++ in science.

I'll eat the fruit at lunch today. If there's no fruit, I'll eat the veggie.

I'll get better at kickball.

I'll write a letter to Grandpa while I'm eating my after-school snack.

In the hall today, I'll say hi to three people I've never said hi to before.

I'll write the best poem I've ever written in my whole life.

I'll stop picking on people.

I'm going to start exercising.

By the end of the year, I'll be a way better student.

I'll take a 20-minute bike ride this Saturday.

By tomorrow, I'll have the cleanest room in the history of the world.

Answers: All the green goals are stinkers. They aren't SMART enough.

Things to Do Before you Bite the Dust

Try making a *life list*—a list of dream-come-true things you'd love to do someday. Think about it: A life list could change your life for the way, way, way, *way* better.

1. walk on the moon

2. make friends in 20 countries

3. find a cure for cancer

4. climb Mt. Everest

5. learn to speak another language

6. sail around the world

7. run a marathon

8. fly a small plane (or a big jet)

9, 10... 100...

A man named John Goddard was 15 years old when he wrote his life list. He listed 127 goals like "climb Mt. Kilimanjaro," "write a book," and "learn to play the violin." So far, he has reached more than 100 of his goals. (You can read more about John and his list at www.johngoddard.info.) Your list of goals can be like his or be completely your own. See how many goals you can come up with now, and add to your list over time. Having a list like this is MOTIVATING. It can make you feel good about getting things done.

Pete, Repeat: The Story Continues*

"YIKES!" Pete said as he woke. "The math test!"

* It started on page 5.

His stomach sank as he realized he hadn't studied. He thought hard about what he should do.

Fake sick? Nope, already did that last week.

Excuse myself to go to the restroom during the test and stay a really long time? Nah, the teacher would send someone to find me.

Tell the teacher we had a family emergency and had to go to the hospital and I forgot to bring my math book with me and we got home so late I never had time to open the book and…. No, she'd never believe it.

As he considered his problem, Pete realized he felt *very* strange. "Something's different," he thought. "I'm… moving…so…so…slow…."

He looked down and *aaaack!* noticed he was green. He had four stubby green legs and a flat green stomach. Something was weird about his back—it felt big and round, like a *shell*.

"What's happened to me?" he cried. "I'm all turtle-y!"

He tried to rise from his bed, but the shell made things difficult. He wiggled and struggled until he finally fell on the floor with a thud. There he was, on his back with his legs and arms waving in the air, when his little sister Patty appeared in the doorway.

"Peter," she said in her bossiest voice, "you're late for breakfast *again*. Mom says get dressed."

He looked at her in amazement. "Doesn't she notice I'm different?" he wondered. "Well," he replied, "excuse *me*, but how am I supposed to get dressed with a big *shell* on my back?"

Patty gave him a bored expression.

"Hel-*lo*, I'm a *turtle*," he said.

"Well, everybody knows that. You're a staller and a slowpoke, and you always *have* been. The bus comes in 5 minutes." She skipped off.

Peter couldn't believe his situation. His sweatshirt ripped when he pulled it over his shell. When he plodded down the stairs, one by one, and crawled to the breakfast table, his parents didn't bat an eye. On the bus, his big shell took up one whole seat. When he tried to open his math book for some last-minute studying, his stubby arms couldn't turn the pages. And when he tried to rush into school to ask his buddies what might be on the test, he . . . couldn't . . . seem . . . to . . . catch . . . up. . . .

Other students whizzed past him in the hall. When he finally made it to class, the test had already begun. The teacher wasn't pleased he was late. "You'll just have to work faster," she said.

Peter tried to hold his pencil but dropped it. The clock was ticking. He could hear the sound of pencils flying across the page, and he knew he'd never finish his test before the bell rang. The teacher would give him an F, his parents would be disappointed, and little Patty would roll her eyes and smirk.

It was useless. Peter pulled his head and arms and legs into his shell. "I wish I'd never procrastinated!" he moaned to himself. The inside of the shell echoed like a cave, bouncing the words around and around: "I wish I'd never procrastinated!

procrastinated!

procrastinated!"

Peter woke with a start. He glanced at the clock and saw it was six o'clock in the morning. Then he looked down and realized, with total relief, that he wasn't a turtle after all. What a nightmare!

He decided to get up and study. He turned on the lights and sat at his desk, thinking, "If I put in an hour now, I can get a lot done. Then I'll eat breakfast and review a little more. If I still need extra time, I'll study on the bus."

Peter felt satisfied. No one was going to call *him* a staller or a slowpoke. And from now on, he'd always remember to be really, really nice to turtles.

How to Stop Procrastinating, Starting Right Now

Get up and do ONE task you've been putting off. You'll feel energized, and you'll be able to say "I did it!" Even if it's just a small thing, you'll know you've accomplished it. That can give you motivation to do another task, and another…and before you know it, you'll be saying "See you later, procrastinator!"

Notes

The facts about procrastination on page 3 were reported in "The Nature of Procrastination: A Meta-Analytic and Theoretical Review of Quintessential Self-Regulatory Failure" by Piers Steel in *Psychological Bulletin,* Vol. 133, No. 1 (January 2007), pp. 65–94. Washington, DC: American Psychological Association.

"Big Project? Break It Down" on pages 72–74 is adapted from *School Power: Study Skill Strategies for Succeeding in School* by Jeanne Shay Schumm, Ph.D. (Minneapolis: Free Spirit Publishing, 2001). Used with permission.

"Don't Be a Blockhead" on pages 76–77 is adapted from *Life Lists for Teens* by Pamela Espeland (Minneapolis: Free Spirit Publishing, 2003). Used with permission.

"Pete, Repeat: The Story Continues" on pages 90–93 was inspired in part by Franz Kafka's short story "Metamorphosis." Sincere apologies to Mr. Kafka.

Index

About the Authors

Pamela Espeland and Elizabeth Verdick have written many books for children and teens including *Dude, That's Rude! (Get Some Manners)*. They both live in Minnesota with their families and pets. They went to the same college, but not at the same time, and they hardly ever miss a deadline.

Other Great Books from Free Spirit

Speak Up and Get Along!
by Scott Cooper

A handy toolbox of ways to get along with others, this book presents 21 strategies kids can learn and use to express themselves, build relationships, end arguments and fights, halt bullying, and beat unhappy feelings. Includes a note to adults. For ages 8–12.
Softcover; 128 pp.; two-color; illust.; 6" x 9"

The Step-Tween Survival Guide
by Lisa Cohn and Debbie Glasser, Ph.D.

Step-tweens are not only caught between childhood and teenhood—they're also often caught between two parents, two families, and two homes. This book helps tweens gain the skills and inspiration to both survive and thrive in a stepfamily. For ages 9–12.
Softcover; 128 pp.; two-color; illust.; 6" x 9"

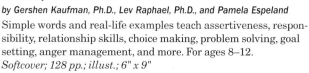

Stick Up for Yourself!
by Gershen Kaufman, Ph.D., Lev Raphael, Ph.D., and Pamela Espeland

Simple words and real-life examples teach assertiveness, responsibility, relationship skills, choice making, problem solving, goal setting, anger management, and more. For ages 8–12.
Softcover; 128 pp.; illust.; 6" x 9"

Fighting Invisible Tigers
(Revised & Updated Third Edition)
by Earl Hipp

This book offers proven techniques that teens can use to deal with stressful situations in school, at home, and among friends. A great resource for any teen who's said, "I'm stressed out!" For ages 11 & up.
Softcover; 144 pp.; two-color; illust.; 6" x 9"

100 Things Guys Need to Know
by Bill Zimmerman

Advice for guys on issues from family life to fitting in, emotions, bullies, school, peer pressure, failure, anger, and more. Graphic-novel-style illustrations, quotes from boys, survey results, facts, and stories keep them interested. Conversation starters for adults are available as a free download at our Web site. For boys ages 9–13.
Softcover; 128 pp.; two-color; illust.; 8" x 10½"

Free Spirit's
Laugh & Learn™ Series

Solid information, a kid-centric point of view, and a sense of humor combine
to make each book in our Laugh & Learn series an invaluable tool for getting
through life's rough spots. For ages 8–13. *Softcover; 72–136 pp.; illust.; 5⅛" x 7"*

Interested in purchasing multiple quantities and receiving volume discounts?
Contact edsales@freespirit.com or call 1.800.735.7323 and ask for Education Sales.

**Many Free Spirit authors are available for speaking engagements, workshops, and
keynotes.** Contact speakers@freespirit.com or call 1.800.735.7323.

www.freespirit.com

Fast, Friendly, and Easy to Use
www.freespirit.com

Browse the catalog

Info & extras

Many ways to search

Quick check-out

Stop in and see!

1.800.735.7323 • fax 612.337.5050 • help4kids@freespirit.com